May 13, 1965 – 1996

Katie,

Thirty-one wonderful years!
Each a year to remember, but
never one quite like this one.

All our love,

Mom

... me
the serenity to
accept the things
I cannot change,
courage to change
the things I can,
and wisdom
to know the
difference.

# Meditations and Positive Thoughts
## for
# Pregnancy & Birth

# Meditations and Positive Thoughts for Pregnancy & Birth

GILLI MOORHAWK

PIATKUS

First published in 1994 by
Judy Piatkus (Publishers) Ltd
5 Windmill Street, London W1P 1HF

**The moral right of the author
has been asserted**

*A catalogue record for this book is available
from the British Library*

ISBN 0-7499-1395-9

Designed by Zena Flax
Artwork by Tracy Rich

Set in Goudy Old Style and Raleigh by
Action Typesetting Limited, Northgate Street, Gloucester
Printed and bound in Great Britain by
Bookcraft Ltd, Midsomer Norton, Avon

This book is dedicated to
midwives everywhere
and in particular Daphne, Diana and Mel
on Community Midwifery at St George's, Tooting
and to Liberty — my inspiration.

# Contents

# Introduction

∿∿∿ Nurturing a baby and giving birth have been very devalued in our society for many years. The natural process of pregnancy and birth has been increasingly medicalised. It is wonderful to see that the pendulum is now swinging back towards a more natural approach. Women are increasingly exploring the options of labour without drugs, active childbirth, water birth and home birth; making their own choices about what is happening to their bodies during this important time.

In addition to making choices about your physical wellbeing, you can also improve your mental and emotional wellbeing by focusing on positive and joyful images. If you study the thoughts that flick through your mind during the day, you will be surprised to see how many negative, and how few positive statements you make – 'I'm too fat', 'I'm useless at this', 'I look tired', 'I've forgotten that'. When did you last say 'How gorgeous I look today'? This book helps you to change your thinking so that you include many more positive statements in your thoughts. There are several simple meditations to use, and dozens of positive statements or affirmations to help you during pregnancy and the weeks leading up to the birth of your baby.

Research shows that the unborn baby is aware of its

environment at a much earlier time than was previously imagined. Since many mood changes are controlled by hormones, and your baby shares your bodily environment, it is now believed that your mood changes will be experienced by the baby. So, if you feel happy and peaceful, your baby will too!

This book encourages you to foster positive thoughts and images around being a mother, the bodily changes that accompany pregnancy, the growth of the baby, and life in general. It also sets the stage for beginning the relationship between mother and child, the relationship that starts at conception and will continue for life.

You only need a few minutes a day, perhaps while travelling to work, in the evening before sleeping, or in bed before you get up in the morning, to start surrounding your child with love and light, encouraging a beautiful and joyful pregnancy and birth.

*Meditations and Positive Thoughts for Pregnancy and Birth* is divided into three sections, one for each of the three terms or trimesters of pregnancy: 0–3 months, 3–6 months and 6 months to birth. However, you can use affirmations from Section Three in the early part of your pregnancy, or affirmations from Section One just before you give birth. Follow your intuition and do what feels right for you. There are meditations on various subjects linked to pregnancy and birth and you may wish to do these as the weeks pass.

The first meditation 'Creating Your Garden', will help to calm your mind and body. You are more receptive to positive thoughts when you are in a relaxed frame of mind. Once you are familiar with the exercise you will find it easy to relax and then work on your chosen affirmation for the day. You may wish to use this meditation every day before working on your particular thoughts, or, if you are familiar with using affirmations, you may prefer to compile a list of thoughts to read every day or write affirmations on cards and carry these around with you. You could try pinning up cards in your home so that they catch your eye throughout the day. The 'Garden' meditation can also be used if you are feeling tired or under stress. Imagine sitting in the beautiful surroundings, feeling the warmth of the sun on your skin. If you are already familiar with meditation and have your own favourite method of relaxing then it is fine to use your normal method.

There are no right or wrong ways to work with positive thoughts. It is not important to remember the affirmations word for word, just hold the thought in your mind and imagine the feelings that surround each one. You can work with one affirmation every day, or four or five daily for a week; do whatever feels best for you.

To affirm literally means to make firm and that is the state of mind required for the best effect of this work. Be firm with your thoughts, weed out the negative thoughts, promote and repeat the positive ones. Expect and accept only the best in your life and you will be amazed at the results you achieve.

Now you are ready to begin.

# *Creating Your Garden*

⟵⟶ Sit down in a comfortable position with your back straight and supported, your hands in your lap and allow your eyes to close. Take a few slow deep breaths and tell yourself that with each breath you become more relaxed and that all the external noises around you only serve to make you feel more and more relaxed.

Now begin to squeeze the tension out of your body by clenching your toes tightly as you breathe in and letting go as you slowly breathe out — try to make the out-breath last twice as long as the in-breath. Breathe in and clench your toes up again, as tightly as you can, then slowly breathe out and feel the tension oozing away from your toes. Feel how relaxed your feet now feel. Now flex your feet at the ankle holding as you breathe in, and letting go as you breathe out. Feel the relaxation flowing up through your knees into your hips — you may find it easier to 'see' the feeling of relaxation as a colour and watch it flowing up through your legs like water.

Now clench your fingers on the in-breath and release on the out-breath, repeat and feel the relaxation flowing from your hands up through your wrists, into your elbows and shoulders. Imagine the relaxing feeling flowing up from your legs and up from your arms and meeting in the centre of your chest, so your breathing is the focus of your attention.

Finally imagine light and relaxation pouring down through the top of your head and relaxing the muscles around your eyes, and in your jaw and down into your chest.

Your whole body is now completely relaxed and your attention is focused in the centre of your chest.

Now let this focus slip down your body until your attention is directed just below your navel. You may wish to increase the contact by placing your hands on your belly and linking with the baby growing within you.

Imagine you are sitting in a garden on a beautiful summer's day. Imagine you can feel the warmth of the sun streaming around you. Relax in the luxurious warmth of the sun. Look around the garden, you may see a wall or a fence around the garden which keeps out any intrusion, or it may be that the garden is so large that you cannot see the boundaries. There may be trees around you, or low shrubs, colourful flowers, or just greenery. Use all your imagination to create the garden which is perfect and individual to you. The sky is brilliant blue and fluffy clouds float by, adding to your feeling of relaxation. You feel completely secure.

Now allow the words or images created by your chosen thought or affirmation to fill your mind and gently repeat them over and over again. Or focus on the images created by the thought and hold them in your mind.

Continue to work with these thoughts and images for as long as you feel comfortable. Then, before you end the session, imagine a bubble of perfect white light forming around the body of your baby, protecting and nurturing your growing child. Now gradually return your awareness to your body, stretch your arms and legs and open your eyes.

# The First
# Trimester

# The First Trimester
## (from 0–3 months)

The first three months of your pregnancy will see the baby growing from an egg the size of a pinhead to a complete foetus containing billions of cells. At three months old the baby has formed all the major organ systems, is around 12 cm (about 5 inches) in length and weighs about 100g (4 ounces). This incredible rate of growth will never be repeated again during the life of your baby. At twelve weeks the baby is over 100,000 times larger than the fertilised egg.

Such momentous changes will have a dramatic impact upon your body too. The flood of new hormones in the bloodstream can cause nausea and morning sickness in the first few weeks. The dramatic demands on your body for raw materials to build the body of your baby may leave you feeling tired and drained. Emotional mood swings can also add more pressure at a time when few people may know of your pregnancy and will not be making allowances for the great changes occurring in your life.

Your breasts may become larger and highly sensitive — you may feel you need to start wearing a bra during the day if you don't normally wear one, and you may be more comfortable wearing a sleep bra at night too. You may also find you become bloated or have lower abdominal or lower back twinges. If you are worried about any of your symptoms, contact your doctor immediately so that your mind can be put at rest.

Discovering you are pregnant, even if you have planned your baby, will bring a whole flood of fearful thoughts. You may wonder if you will be able to cope, what people will say, if the things you are experiencing are common and you may worry about money and the wellbeing of your baby. It is very reassuring to know that such fears are common. The thoughts and meditations in this first section will focus mainly on replacing these common negative thoughts and fears with positive life-enhancing affirmations.

I visualise a beautiful,
tranquil pregnancy
and a problem-free birth.

I feel fulfilled
as my baby grows
within me.

I easily change my lifestyle
to ensure I am
in perfect health to nurture
my baby.

I feel great about
being pregnant.

# I love my baby unconditionally.

# I am gentle with myself and allow myself time to adjust to all the changes in my body.

I now give myself
permission to rest and relax
when my body is tired.
It is OK to do nothing.

I feel safe and secure
at all times,
my partner and friends are
supportive and loving.

I nurture myself
and my body as
I undergo the changes
of pregnancy.

I have the best care
from my doctor and midwife,
they make me feel secure.

# My baby grows perfectly
# and healthily
# within me.

# Giving birth
# is a joyful event.

# I feel beautiful.

# Meditation for Conception

～～～ This meditation can be done before you conceive, when you discover you are pregnant, or when you first feel the baby moving within you. Sit down facing your partner in a space that you have made special, with some beautiful flowers, roses if possible — and candlelight. Before sitting to meditate, prepare some oil in a small dish by mixing two drops of rose absolute into two teaspoons of almond or grapeseed oil and place the dish between you where you sit. The dish should preferably be beautiful to look at, of delicate china, glass or crystal.

Dipping your fingers into the oil, you and your partner take turns to anoint the other, first on the forehead, then at the heart, then below the navel, and finally on the palm of each hand. At the forehead this is done with the intent of focusing thought on the child-to-be, at the heart with the intent of offering that child love, on the belly with the intent of nurturing the child and on the hands with the intent of welcoming the child into the world. The intentions can be voiced aloud or held in the mind. During the rest of the meditation you may either sit holding hands or the man may place one hand on the woman's belly. This is particularly appropriate if the meditation is to mark the baby's first movement within the womb.

Now see a beam of rose-coloured light flowing from your heart to your partner's heart, forming the base of a triangle and another beam flowing upwards to form the apex of the triangle above your heads. Slowly feel yourself being drawn up to the top of the triangle and invite the incoming soul into this space. From the depth of your hearts call out to this being with the love you already feel for it, your desire to welcome this soul into your lives and your intent to nurture and care for it. Then remain for some time with these feelings of great love and happiness, before slowly and gently returning your awareness to the present time and the place where you are sitting.

Adapted from a meditation in *Subtle Aromatherapy* by Patricia Davis by kind permission of C W Daniel Company Limited.

I honour and send love
to the incoming soul
who chooses
to be with us.

Bearing a child brings
great joy to all.

All is well.

My body was created
to give birth perfectly
and my pregnancy
will be perfect.

I am ready to embrace
motherhood.

# *Meditation for Linking With Your Baby*

〜〜〜 Once you learn that you are pregnant you can easily and effortlessly link with your baby as it grows within you. Your baby is sensitive to your moods and emotions from around four months' gestation and will respond to your love and attention.

Sit or lie in a comfortable position and close your eyes. Allow your body to relax as you concentrate on your breathing. You may wish to rest your hands on your belly to increase your sense of contact with your baby. As you continue to relax, bring your awareness to your belly and the new life growing within you. You may see the baby as a light, or as a form, or just be aware of a presence — however you view the baby is fine. Just hold the image in your mind and talk to your baby, either silently or out loud, sending them your love, and tell them how much you are looking forward to sharing your life with them. Talk to them about the birth you plan and how you see them fitting into your life. Talk about the characteristics you feel are important for a person to have, being courageous, warm and loving, generous, calm and any other virtues you can think of. Allow any responses in the shape of feelings, colours or images to form in your mind and be joyful and playful in your communications. Talk about your life, your hopes and dreams — communicate with your child as you would with a close friend on the end of the telephone.

When you have finished your conversation surround the baby in a protective bubble of light, using whichever colour feels most suitable. See this light expand, enclosing both of you with calm and peace for the rest of the day.

When you are ready, open your eyes and return to normal consciousness.

Repeat this meditation as often as you wish.

I send love
to the baby
growing inside me.

Every time
I think of my baby
I surround us both
with love and light.

I know I will be
a wonderful mother
to my baby.

I focus completely
on the joy
of my pregnancy.

I follow my intuition
and the messages
from my body
as they indicate
the changes I need to make
in my lifestyle
for the perfect support
of my baby.

Our baby has chosen
to be with us
and we look forward
to meeting and
loving
our baby.

Everything in my life
now resolves in a perfect way
for my highest good.

My baby is
perfectly supported
by my body.

I feel beautiful and radiant
and enjoy the changes
occurring in my body.

# The Second
Trimester

# The Second Trimester
## (from 3–6 months)

〜〜〜〜 During the second term many women feel wonderful. Morning sickness and nausea will usually have passed and you can start to enjoy your pregnancy. Your waist may be thickening but as yet you won't be carrying too much extra weight. Your energy levels are high and you generally feel very well. Your hair and skin may be at their best and you will develop the healthy glow that pregnant women seem to have. This is a good time to take a holiday if you can, but be careful not to overdo things and remember to rest as much as you can.

The baby is completely formed at twelve weeks, so the focus during this period is maturation and growth; the nervous system, skeletal and other systems mature, and by the end of the second term the baby will be around 33cm (13 inches) long and weigh 500g (1¼ pounds).

You will start to feel the baby moving during this time – generally around 18 to 20 weeks in a first pregnancy, a little earlier in later pregnancies. This is very exciting and may be when you really start to relate to this new person growing inside you. Early movements are slight and barely noticeable, but will soon develop into definite kicks, which may tickle!

Many women have very vivid dreams during the second term – and this is believed to be one way of dealing with any anxieties or feelings about the pregnancy in a safe and secure way. You may find it helpful to write your dreams down as this will allow you to reflect on any subconscious fears you were previously unaware of.

Recent research shows that the baby has acute hearing by around four months' gestation, so you may enjoy talking to the baby, or singing (the baby won't criticise even the worst singing voice − don't worry!). Your normal daily conversations are a part of the baby's environment, as well as your heartbeat and the sounds of your breathing and digestive system. These are all familiar and reassuring to him or her. You can also involve your partner by asking him to read stories to the baby. The baby will begin to recognise his voice and will respond to him in the months ahead. It is important to remember that fathers are expecting a baby too and a night-time story-telling ritual can help to strengthen the bonds between the three of you. At the end of this book you will find suggestions for stories to read to your unborn child.

I feel beautiful and
enjoy being pregnant.

The first movements
of my baby
are a source of great joy
for me.

I take time every day
to sit quietly
and talk
to my baby.

I experience
great inner peace
throughout my pregnancy.
I am calm and tranquil
at all times.

My baby and I grow
more in tune
with every passing day.

I am radiant and beautiful
as I nurture
the baby within me.

My baby communicates
needs and wants to me
easily and clearly.

Perfection is now unfolding
in my life.

I love the way my body
is growing.
My breasts and my belly
are beautiful.

I feel calm and contented
at all times.
I nurture my baby
easily and effortlessly.

I accept and honour
the physical changes
in my body.

My baby is growing perfectly.

# Meditation for Linking With Your Partner

~~~~~ Pregnancy is a time of great changes. Along with the physical changes in a woman's body come changes on the mental level, to do with becoming a parent. There will also be changes on an emotional level between the mother and father of the baby. Where once there were only two, now there will be three. Few excited parents-to-be can appreciate the enormous changes that a baby will bring into their lives and it can be a shock to discover the responsibilities that accompany your new bundle of joy. This meditation helps to strengthen the bonds of love between the parents, forming a strong, secure partnership to create a firm foundation for the new baby.

Try to wear something pink, burn pink candles, or have something pink, for example a cushion, nearby. Pink is the colour that resonates most with the heart and loving feelings. Read through the meditation with your partner until you are comfortable with the simple steps.

Sit comfortably facing your partner. Take a deep breath, hold it for a moment, then exhale. Repeat twice, and on the third exhalation let all the breath flow from your body and sit in the quietness for a moment before starting to breathe naturally and normally.

Enjoy the peace and calm and focus on the feelings of relaxation between you for a few moments before proceeding. Arrange for one partner to reach over and touch the other partner's hand to signal you are ready to move on to the next step.

Imagine a beam of light flowing from up above you and into the top of your head. Imagine that this light is coming from a distant star and is of the frequency of love. The light is brilliant white, but on contact with your body it becomes a beautiful warm pink colour. The light flows down into your head, and also around the outside of your body, surrounding you both in a protective cocoon of light. This cocoon keeps you both safe and secure and free from any external distractions. Any external noises will serve only to make you feel more calm and relaxed.

Imagine that the light flowing down through your body flows downwards into the ground, anchoring you both to the earth, but linking you only with the clean and pure grounding energies. Allow the light to flow through you, pouring into your head and emerging from your feet and holding you securely to the earth.

Now that you are securely grounded, turn your attention to your heart. Feel the light flowing down into your head and pouring into your heart, filling it with love. As your heart fills with love, it overflows and fills the space between you and your partner. In your mind's eye watch the energies come together and then flow and merge until there is a beautiful ball of loving energy between you. Now the ball forms into two new spheres and the love contained within each circle is a union of the love from each partner. These spheres shrink down in size, becoming more and more concentrated loving energy and then one moves into the heart of each partner.

As the sphere enters your heart feel it expand, filling your whole being with love — love for your partner, love for your baby, and the altruistic love for all people and all things. This love penetrates every cell, every fibre of your being and lifts your thoughts to a higher and more loving frequency. You will find it easier to be loving and peaceful in the weeks ahead. You will find that mistakes or blunders don't upset you the way they used to, and that you can see the good in all things. A new bond of love has been forged between you and your partner and this bond will continue to grow and strengthen in the weeks and months ahead.

Embrace your partner and sit quietly together enjoying these new feelings of love and closeness.

You should do this meditation with your partner once a week from the third month until the birth of the baby, and you may find it useful to continue to link together during the early weeks after the birth.

The love between
my partner and I
grows stronger and deeper
as our baby grows.

A bond of incredible love
forms between
my partner, myself
and our baby.

My partner loves
and supports me
and our baby.

My partner looks forward
to the birth of my baby
and supports all my choices
surrounding the birth.

I accept all the love
and support
that is offered to me
during my pregnancy.

Other people accept
my birth plans
and support my decisions
about my labour and birth.

As my belly grows larger
and my baby kicks within me,
I am filled with
incredible joy.

I now release
all preconceived ideas
about the sex of my baby.
I will be happy with
a girl or a boy.

All areas of my life are
moving towards perfection for the
highest good of all concerned.

# *Meditation for Releasing Your Fears*

⌒⌒⌒ It is perfectly natural for mothers to
experience fleeting fears about the health and wellbeing
of their baby. We live in a world where bad news is
broadcast daily on TV and radio, and printed in
newspapers. It is hard to avoid hearing of sad events and
wonder how we would cope in the same situation. During
pregnancy, when you are feeling emotionally open and
vulnerable, it is all too easy to over-react to small fears
and concerns and for them to take hold in your mind,
causing yet more anxiety.

This meditation will help you to clear away any fears
and anxieties that may be upsetting you. These may be
distant fears, brought on by exposure to bad news, or fears
due to your own birth experience or the experiences of
someone in your family.

Sit or lie in a comfortable position and close your eyes.
Take a deep breath and feel any tension flowing out of
your body as you exhale. Take another deep breath and
feel your body becoming more and more relaxed.
Continue to focus on your breath until you feel calm
and centred.

Now imagine a stream of white light flowing into your
body through the top of your head. As the light enters
your body it washes all the fears and anxieties from every

cell in your body. The light moves down through your head, and your eyes, your ears, your nose, and your mouth are all cleansed and cleared of any fear.

The light moves down into your neck clearing your throat and larynx, then into your shoulders and down through your elbows, wrists and hands, until the light streams out of your fingertips. The light continues down into your heart and lungs and each and every cell of your body is cleansed and cleared. No fears or negative images remain. Your stomach, liver and intestines, your kidneys and all the other organs in your abdomen are cleansed and cleared and the waves of white light continue to stream down through your body, lifting all these fears out of every cell. Now move your awareness down to your pelvis and watch the light cleanse and clear any negativity around your uterus and pelvis and streams of light wash down through your pelvis and down through your legs, your knees and ankles and out of your toes.

Now imagine a wave of beautiful blue light starting to pour into the top of your head. This light picks up the negative thoughts and emotions that have been released by the white light and carries them away for ever, transforming them into clear white light and returning them to the Universal Source, God, the Universe, the Light or whatever concept you feel happiest with. This beautiful blue light washes every remnant of fear and anxiety away from your body, and soothes and heals any areas of your body which have been hurt or bruised by these negative emotions.

Once the blue light has streamed through your whole

body, a new ray of light appears, this time it is a beautiful calming pink colour. This pink light replaces all the negative emotions with positive images of love and health and perfection. As this pink light pours through your body repeat the following:

'I now release all negative thoughts and images concerning birth and the health and perfection of my baby. These thoughts and images are not relevant for my birth and my baby and I now replace them with thoughts of perfection. My baby will be born in perfect health at full term, in the perfect place and we will both be surrounded by loving and supportive people during the process of birth. I now affirm for a perfect birth for my baby and I.'

See how the pink light fills your body and radiates outwards so you are surrounded by light. This light will keep you protected and safe from any negative thoughts and images.

Now when you are ready, open your eyes and return to normal consciousness.

Repeat this meditation as often as you wish.

I now release
any negative feelings
that no longer uplift
or nurture me.

I now acknowledge any fears
and anxieties I have
about being pregnant
and becoming a mother.
These fears are normal.

My baby is protected
from any negative experiences
or emotions I may have
during my pregnancy.

I listen to my inner knowing
and I am in tune
with the needs of my baby.

My baby and I
are held in the light
at all times.
We are safe from any upset
or distress.

Birth is
a natural process.

I see myself
in radiant health
throughout my pregnancy.

I enjoy seeing my body change
as my baby grows
within me.

I am a wonderful mother.

I am calm and content.
I release all worries
and thoughts
that upset me.

My baby is calm,
happy and contented.

My baby has a strong
and healthy body
and is perfect in all ways.

I release all memories
and images of imperfect
birth experiences
and replace them
with positive nurturing images.

My baby is growing perfectly,
physically, mentally,
emotionally and spiritually.

I now release fears
and problems from the past
and look forward
to the future
with my baby.

All problems in my life
resolve before my
baby is born.

I surround my baby with love
at all times.

# Meditation for Abundance

⁓⁓⁓  One thing is for certain — babies are expensive! The cost of prams, cots, nappies, and a never-ending stream of clothes in the first few months would put a strain on any purse, but added to the loss of one income if the mother leaves work to have the baby, it can seem impossible to make ends meet.

This thought is all-pervasive in most couples. However, talk to anyone who has had a baby and they will all agree on one thing — *Babies Bring Abundance*. Even people who perhaps didn't plan the baby and had not made financial provisions for their new arrival will tell you that somehow money always turned up. You will find you receive gifts from people you hardly know, presents from relatives you haven't seen in twenty years, loans of prams and other equipment from family and friends, neighbours, workmates, and even friends of friends. Goodwill, love and blessings from all around the world will shower on you and your new baby.

Additional sources of income will appear to you in the weeks and months after the birth of your baby, new opportunities in your career, new business options, new ideas and new contacts will all be available, if you are open to the possibilities. You will find that other mothers are perhaps not as keen to return to full-time employment, and they too will be looking for ways to earn money from home. Between you, you will find a whole world of potential to improve your abundance.

If you start believing that abundance is your birthright, that you deserve to have money and financial security, then the money will start to trickle into your bank account. People often say that they feel guilty about asking for money when people are poor, or homeless, or starving. It is a little known fact that if the entire wealth of the world were divided out to every man, woman and child on this planet, then each person would be a millionaire. All you are asking for is your share and if you have money you have the ability to pass it on to people *you* feel are needy. Many people give one-tenth of their income, or even just one-tenth of their unexpected income to charities or deserving causes, thus further affirming their own abundance.

Believe that you deserve financial security and affirm that fact daily and you will be amazed how money starts to flow into your life.

Use the 'Garden' meditation to calm and relax you and then imagine that you are feeling really secure and safe. Know that all your financial needs will be met, that money will come to you whenever you need it. Hold whatever thought or image best represents this financial security to you during the day and call that image to mind whenever you have feelings or anxieties around money.

# Money to support my baby will come easily.

# As my baby grows within me my external abundance grows too.

Everything I want and need
to best support my baby
manifests in my life now.

All is well.
Everything proceeds for
the highest good
of all concerned.

# The Third
# Trimester

# The Third Trimester
# (from 6–9 months)

~~~~~ Now you are in the final weeks of your
pregnancy. Soon you will be meeting your baby for the
first time. You may start to feel more unwieldy as your
baby grows bigger and bigger, and during this time it is
very important to ensure you have enough rest and
relaxation to help your body deal with the excess weight.
Gentle exercises can help prepare your body for the
rigours of labour and there are many natural remedies
recommended to help prepare your uterus.

Raspberry leaf, either in tablet form or as tea, is good
for strengthening the uterus and one cup should be drunk
daily after 36 weeks. Some homeopathic remedies can also
be used with good effect. Arnica 30 can be taken during
labour and after the birth as it relieves bruising, both
physical and emotional. Rescue Remedy is another
natural remedy which is often used. You should put
2 drops in a glass of water which can be sipped between
contractions; repeat as necessary throughout labour.
Consult your midwife or alternative health therapist
before using these remedies.

Thoughts and fears about labour and birth may arise
during this period and it is important that you get
reassurance from your midwife and doctor or from friends
and family. Talk to your mother about your own birth and

write down how you feel about this. Remember that many women, because of their different shaped bodies, have different experiences in labour, so try to get a broad range of experiences. Reading about other women's experiences can be reassuring, and you will find a recommended reading list at the end of this book.

Try to rub oil into your stomach and breasts every day. This will help to stop stretch marks and also bring you into contact with your baby. During this period the shape of the baby can be felt through the abdominal wall and you may feel him or her responding to your stroking.

Ensure you maintain good eating habits during the last three months, even though you may find you can't eat as much as you used to because your stomach is compressed with the growing baby inside you. Heartburn can also be a problem, but this can be helped by eating several small regular meals during the day.

As the weeks pass, bringing you closer to your labour, you can really begin to look forward to the birth of your baby.

I am now ready
to be a mother.

Pregnancy is a
natural state of being.
My body can give birth
to my baby easily.

My birth will be
a wonderful and joyful event
as I meet my baby
for the first time.

The birth of our baby
brings true perfection
into our lives.

Birth is a beautiful,
natural process.

My baby will choose
the ideal time to be born for
his or her highest purpose.

All my preparations
are complete.
I can now relax and enjoy
the last few weeks of
my pregnancy.

# Meditation for Love

As the birth of your child draws near, you may think a lot about love. You may worry that you won't have enough love to go around. Will you still have enough love for your partner and your friends? Can you possibly love your second child as much as you love your first? Such worries, however, are groundless. Love is an infinite resource; the more love you give, the more love you have to give. And for a baby, love is very, very important. Without love, an otherwise healthy baby will sicken. A baby that is loved will blossom in the most difficult conditions.

Sometimes it takes a little time for love to flow from mother to new baby. Reasons for this can be a difficult or premature birth, problems with breastfeeding, or a baby who is fussy and crying. Instead of the rush of love you expected, you find you don't really feel anything towards this new person in your life. Many mothers feel this way in the first few days; the overwhelming experience of giving birth can leave you emotionally drained and it takes a little time to recover.

The following meditation will help you to open your heart and encourage the love between you and your baby. You can do the meditation at any time during pregnancy, and it may be very useful to do it just before birth and again in the days following the birth of your baby. If you do the meditation after the birth ask your partner to read it to you, perhaps while you are sitting down feeding the baby.

Sit or lie in a comfortable position and allow your body to relax. Feel your breathing settle into a calm and leisurely flow; gently inhaling and exhaling. Just watch your breath, don't try to control it, just watch as it slows and deepens, deeper and slower, and you feel very calm and relaxed.

Now imagine you are standing outside your body, and see yourself shrinking down until you are very tiny. Now look at your body and imagine you can fly into your heart. Feel yourself flying through your skin and into your body and find yourself in a small room inside your heart. As you walk into the room you find that on every side of you are taps, big bath taps, rows and rows of them. You look at the first tap and see that it has your partner's name written on it and flowing from the tap is a stream of pure love. Look at the tap and see whether it is as fully open as it can be, if not, turn the tap until it is full on and watch the love flow out clearly and cleanly. Now move on to the next tap and see which name is written on it. Perhaps it will be a parent, a brother or sister or a friend. Look at the tap and maybe this time you will see that the tap is just dripping, or only a small stream is flowing from it. You may sense that the stream seems to be the wrong colour for that person or maybe the tap isn't flowing at all. Turn the tap and watch the stream of love flow outwards, changing in speed and colour until it is just right for that person.

Now walk along until you find the tap which has been set aside for your baby. There may not be a name on it yet, but you know that this tap holds all the love for your baby. See how the love is flowing from the tap; it may be flowing freely and clear and bright, or it may be a little slow. You may find that the tap is slightly stiff as you try to turn it because it hasn't been used much. So turn the tap around and around until it is full on, and the stream of love is flowing well and know that love is now flowing perfectly between you and your child.

Now continue along the row and check that all the taps are working correctly. You may be surprised that some taps aren't working too well, and others you had thought would be in need of attention are working perfectly. Make any adjustments or corrections you feel are necessary and then continue walking along until you reach the unmarked taps. You see rows and rows of taps that are unnamed and switched off. These are the taps for people who will be important in your life in the future. Friends you will meet during your lifetime. Children you will bear, friends of your children and children of your friends. The potential you have to love is enormous and your capacity to love is limitless.

Now walk back to the door, taking one last look at this source of love, knowing that all is well in your heart. Then fly out of your body and feel yourself getting larger and larger until you are your normal size. Then come back into your body and, when you are ready, open your eyes.

The birth of my baby
brings unlimited love
into my life.

I see the highest good
in all the people around me.

My heart expands with love.

Motherhood makes me
a peaceful
and loving woman.

I expect the best
and I receive the best
in all areas of my life.

The more I give love,
the more love I have to give.

# My partner is more loving as we welcome our baby into our family.

# Love is abundant in my life.

My baby is a loving presence
in my life.

I have unlimited reserves
of love to share.

Now I am a mother
I have even more love
to give to others.

My heart is open
to receive all the love
that is offered to me.

Every child I bear
brings more love
into my life.

I allow love for myself,
I am infinitely lovable.

The best gift
I can give my baby
is my love.

# Love surrounds me – always.

I try to do
everything in my life
in the spirit of love.

# Labour and Birth

～～～ First-time mothers are often worried that they won't know when they are in labour. But unless you are one of the minority who have a very fast and painless labour, you will notice one or more symptoms. Your waters may break, you may have diarrhoea or backache and notice irregular cramp-like pains, but these may precede the onset of labour by hours or days, or you may have a bloodstained show. If you start experiencing abdominal pains that are regular and increasing in frequency, this is a good indication that labour is beginning. It is helpful to start timing the interval between these pains, and if they start to become more intense and closer together you should consult your doctor or midwife. Once labour is well established it is certainly not something you can overlook!

In the early hours of labour it is wise to try to rest. You should sleep if you can, though excitement generally makes that difficult, especially if it's your first baby. Just lying down in bed, however, will help you to conserve your energy. In the hours before labour becomes so intense that your focus is completely inward, you may wish to do the following meditations and read some of the affirmations that follow.

# Flower Meditation

Take a deep breath in and as you exhale feel all the tension in your body flowing away. Inhale again, imagining clear white light entering your lungs as you do so, and let any darkness or negativity flow out with each out-breath.

When you feel relaxed and centred, visualise a flower bud floating in the air before you. As you watch, a ray of light bathes the flower and slowly, petal by petal, it begins to open. When the flower is fully open you see sitting within it a beautiful baby. Imagine you hold out your hands to the baby and it floats towards you. As it does so the petals of the flower begin to close behind it until the flower is once more a closed bud and the light that surrounded the flower and encouraged it to open and grow now surrounds the baby.

Now affirm that when the time comes for your baby to be born, your cervix will open as easily as the flower you just visualised and, once the baby is born and the birth process is complete, the cervix will close, just like the flower. This process is perfect and natural and it will be so with your birth.

When you are in labour imagine your cervix is the flower and spend a few moments every hour visualising the cervix opening to allow the passage of your baby.

Imagine the light bathing your cervix and warming and energising your pelvic area, so that all the muscles and tissues are able to work at perfect efficiency to aid the birth of your baby. After the placenta is delivered, hold the image of the closed flower bud in your mind for a few moments, reminding your body that this is the perfect way for your cervix to be.

My baby is born perfectly
at full-term after
an easy labour.

I am looking forward
to greeting my baby.

My breasts are
perfectly formed
to feed my baby.

I am looking forward
to the birth of my baby.
The birth will be perfect.

I will be able to cope
with my labour easily.

My breasts fill with milk
after the birth
and my baby feeds easily.

My mother supports me
and honours and respects
all my decisions
as a new mother.

My baby is beautiful
within and without.

# *Meditation for the End of Pregnancy*

⌒⌒⌒⌒ Many women feel so wonderful during their pregnancy that they feel an extraordinary sense of loss after the birth of their baby. This wonderful state of being pregnant that has been part of their life for the last nine months is now gone, and it is only natural to miss it.

If you feel this meditation is right for you, I suggest that you do it the day before your due date, or, if the baby is early, do this meditation as soon as possible after the birth.

Sit or lie in a comfortable position and bring your awareness to your breathing. Allow your body to relax with every in-breath and become even more relaxed with each out-breath. When you feel calm and centred allow the image of your body to enter your mind. Allow your mind's eye to view every part of your body that has been affected by your pregnancy. See how thick and luxuriant your hair has become, how full and rounded your breasts, the incredible roundness of your belly nurturing the child within. Send love and affection to this image of your body, the body that has performed the miracle of creating and nurturing new life; the life of the child that you will soon be holding in your arms.

Now look within your body and see the child within. The baby that is now ready to be born. Focus on the baby that your body has so perfectly nurtured, and release the attachment to the miracle of your pregnant body. The body has done its job perfectly, and now it is time to take the next step. The baby will be born, and your body will return to its pre-pregnancy form. As you watch your body, see your belly slowly flatten, feel the changes that return your body to normal. Thank your body for the perfection of your pregnancy, for nurturing your child, for giving you such a wonderful experience in the past nine months and allow it now to return to normal.

Hold the image of your baby in your mind and the picture of your body now returned to normal. Send love and acceptance to this new image and allow the picture to enter your heart. Relax for a while and let yourself feel good about this process. When you feel ready, open your eyes and return to normal consciousness.

Giving birth to my baby
will expand my capacity
to give and receive love.

I see myself
giving birth easily to a
healthy perfect baby.

I feel safe and secure
at all times.

I now release all fears
around labour and birth.
I visualise a perfect birth
for me and my baby.

I now release all attachments
to a particular birth place
or time
and allow my baby
to choose the best place
and time to be born.

I am ready to embrace
motherhood.
I eagerly anticipate
the birth of my baby.

Mothering comes easily to me.

I am successful as a mother.
I nurture my baby with love.

My mother offers me
love and support
as I also become
a mother.

My baby is perfect
in all ways
and copes easily
with the transition
from within me
to the outside world.

My baby knows how to feed
and will do so
in perfect time.

All fears of birthing
are now released.

My baby and I are held
in the light during labour
and we are both kept
in perfect safety
at all times.

My baby's birth will be easy
for both of us.

I am full of light and energy
during the birthing process
and everything goes well.

We are perfectly supported
on all levels
during the birthing.

I am surrounded by loving
and supportive people
during my labour and
at the birth of my baby.

I am surrounded by loving
My baby is born full of joy
and light and
brings happiness into
the lives of all.

# *Ceremony to Welcome Your Baby*

~~~~~ In many societies, the major life passages of birth, puberty, marriage, childbirth and death are marked by ritual and ceremony, but sadly in the West such rites have largely been forgotten. Birth is a time of initiation for the child, but is also an initiation for both the new mother and the new father. Because of the changes in her body, it is obvious that a woman is expecting a baby but it is easy to forget that the father is expecting too. The woman becomes a mother and learns the lessons that her mother before her learned. This transition may mark a new closeness in her relationship with her own mother. The man becomes a father and his own relationship with his father may be brought into view.

A ceremony to mark the birth of your new baby can focus attention on this important time, easing the transition into parenthood and honouring this rite of passage.

Make an area beautiful and welcoming, with flowers, crystals and candles. Place some rose or neroli oil in a burner and fill the air with perfume. If you are doing the meditation with your partner, place the baby on a blanket between you, otherwise put the baby in front of you.

Close your eyes and breathe deeply, allowing your attention to come to your centre. Attain a state of relaxed alertness and allow your attention to focus on your new baby. Imagine a ray of brilliant white light streaming into the baby's head and filling that perfect body with light. See that every cell is filled with light, enhancing and protecting your baby. Watch as the light forms a protective bubble around your baby and know that your child is now held in perfect protection.

Now see a picture of your mother in your mind and her mother, and grandmother and the line of mothers that stretches back through the generations. And see the ties that link all these women in maternity, through pregnancy and childbirth that all have experienced, and see the link pass through you and into your child. Know that the love, nurture and wisdom of the motherline and the feminine line is showering upon you as you make the transition to motherhood and husband of a mother.

Now see a picture of your father and the line of fathers stretching back through the years. See the love, wisdom and strength that passes down through the years to ease your passage into fatherhood and wife of a father.

Hold the hand of your partner and place the other hand on the baby between you. See a brilliant light surrounding all three of you, forging strong bonds between you all as husband and wife, father and child and mother and child. Each relationship is individual and has equal importance. Imagine love pouring from your heart and into the heart of your partner and your child. Again this love forges and strengthens the bonds between you all.

Sit for a few minutes and enjoy the love and radiance that now surrounds you all and know that this peace and is accessible to you all at any time. Now bring your attention back to your surroundings and open your eyes.

My baby has a strong
and healthy body
and is never ill.

My baby is sunny-natured
and loving.

My baby enjoys
the challenges of life
and meets the challenges
easily and effortlessly.

My baby grows up safe
and secure.

We intuitively know
the perfect ways
to help our baby to
adjust to this new reality.

My body returns to
its pre-pregnancy state
easily.

I lose all the extra weight
I have gained
within six weeks of
the birth of my baby.

My baby is calm and peaceful
and has the inner resources
to deal with all
life's challenges
easily and with joy.

Our baby is strong and healthy,
now and always.

# I am transformed
# by the process of birth.

Please write and tell me of your experiences with meditation and affirmation in pregnancy (the address is on page 127, under 'Tapes'). I am also collecting stories from mothers who have had experiences with angels, devas, dolphins, spiritual guides, the soul of their baby and all aspects of the higher realms during their pregnancy and around the time of birth.

I send you love and light as you embark on the journey of motherhood.

# Further Reading

*Spiritual Midwifery* Ina May Gaskin
The Book Publishing Company 1977

*New Active Birth Handbook* Janet Balaskas
Thorsons 1991

*Waterbirth* Janet Balaskas
Thorsons 1992

*The Art of Breastfeeding*
Collins/Angus & Robertson 1990

*Water Babies* Erik Sidenbladh
Adam & Charles Black, 1983

*Magical Child* Joseph Chilton Pearce
Plune 1992

*Birth Reborn* Michel Odent
Fontana 1986

*The Secret Life of the Unborn Child* Thomas Verny with John Kelly
Dell Publishing 1986

*Nurturing the Unborn Child* Thomas Verny and Pamela Weintraub
Dell Publishing 1991

*The Incarnating Child* Joan Salter
Hawthorn Press 1987

*Birth without Violence* Frederick Leboyer
Fontana 1977

*Ideal Birth* Sondra Ray
Celestial Arts 1986

*Subtle Aromatherapy* Patricia Davis
The C W Daniel Co Ltd 1991

*Creative Visualisation* Shakti Gawain
Bantam 1982

*Homeopathy for Mother and Baby* Miranda Castro
Macmillan 1992

*Nature's Child* Leslie Kenton
Ebury Press 1993

# Books to read to your unborn child

*Over the Hills and Far Away*
Floris Books 1991

*Celtic Wonder Tales*
Floris Classics 1988

*Twenty Jataka Tales* Retold by Noor Inayat Khan
East West Publications 1985

*The Tangle Coated Horse* Ella Young
Floris Books 1991

*Primal Myths* Barbara Sproul
HarperCollins 1991

*An Anthology of Sacred Texts by and about Women* Serenity Young
Pandora 1993

*The Puffin Book of 20th Century Children's Verse*
Brian Patten (ed) 1991

*Just So Stories* Rudyard Kipling
Puffin 1987

*Beggars, Beasts and Easter Fire* Carol Greene
Lion 1993

*Angels, Angels All Around* Bob Hartman
Lion 1993

*Worlds of Differences* Martin Palmer and Esther Bisset
Nelson Blackie 1989

*The Lion Children's Bible*
1991

# Tapes

A cassette tape of the meditations in this book, featuring music by
Blair Packham, is available by sending a cheque for £6.99, payable to
One Tiger, to PO Box 3899, London SW12 9XT. Please allow 28
days for delivery. In the US and Canada the cassette is available from
No.1 Imperfects, PO Box 131, 260 Adelaide Street East, Toronto,
Canada MSA 1N1, price US $10.99 or C$12.99. Prices include
postage and packing.

# Useful Addresses

**The Active Birth Centre**
55 Dartmouth Park Road, London NW5 1SL
Telephone 071-267 3006

**Association for the Improvement in Maternity Services (AIMS)**
40 Kingswood Avenue, London NW6 6LS
Telephone 081-960 5585

**Association of Radical Midwives**
62 Greetby Hill, Ormskirk, Lancashire L39 2DT
Telephone 0695-572776

**Independent Midwives Association**
Nightingale Cottage, Shamblehurst Lane, Botley, Hampshire SO3 2BY
Telephone 0703-694429

**National Childbirth Trust**
Alexandra House, Oldham Terrace, London W3 6NH
Telephone 081-992 8637

**Osteopathic Centre for Children (OCC)**
4 Harcourt House, 19a Cavendish Square, London W1M 9AD
Telephone 071-495 1231

Pregnant women and their unborn babies benefit from osteopathy and
the practitioners at the OCC are happy to treat women during their
pregnancy and after the birth. The OCC hopes gradually to establish
post-natal checks for mothers and babies as a normal part of health
care.